The Major Laws

"Quotes that better your mental"

James "Major" Butler

Volume 1

The Major Laws

Copyright © **2020**
James "Major" Butler

Cover Art By Antoine "222" Mitchell.

Executive Editor Shairda Kimoko Brown.

Formatted by Raquel Lewis.

ISBN: 978-0-578-23667-4

For information contact:
James "Major" Butler
Email: themajorlaws@gmail.com
Facebook: James Major Butler
Instagram: @MajorMook

Please visit our website @ www.vintagecoffee37.com
Online Ordering is available for all products.

Dedicated to Brock Singleton

Being the youngest out of five boys, my older cousin Brock is who I looked to for guidance. As a young teen, you were like a God to me. I wanted to talk like you, walk like you and mostly dress like you. You taught me so many things in life and was always there when I needed a hand. I deleted a few sentences that describe your current situation because I know life just happens. The important part for me is to give you the well deserved flowers while you can smell them. Hopefully this dedication can touch you and motivate you to be the gOD you were meant to be.

~Love

FOREWORD

MAJOR /ˈmājər/

Adjective: Important, Serious, or Significant

3 important words. To me those words say, "I ain't come here to play no games. I came here to get some ground breaking shit done." Of course Mook would word that way more politically correct than I could ever, that's just the type of man Major Mook is. He lives by those 3 words, and when you put Major in front of your name there's really no other option.

I've known (Major) Mook for many years, from middle school through high school, and a college semester. Along with being from the same neighborhood , Kenner City (UVC), you know who you know and paths cross often. From then until present day his mission has always been about elevating the music culture. Taking from the lessons left behind by our legends and building upon them to further ourselves as a culture and people.

Many see the culture as a quick come up. Just here to ride the trendy wave and milk it for all that they can. To stand out from the vultures we play individual pivotal roles and display characteristics of cultural integrity, honor, intelligence, and overall good taste. Perfect qualities of someone major.

The culture is often compared to being a lifestyle. Culture is more than lifestyle. It is LIFE. This culture gives lessons to live by from A to Z. Mental health, diet, finance, business, and more are taught within this culture of ours. Our culture is a village. We raise and nurture our own. Teach and feed our own. Show our own how to live a prosperous life and equip them with the tools to do so. This is ours. We live it. We share it. We Major.

-222

ACKNOWLEDGEMENTS

GOD is Great! I will forever be an honorable messenger for your plan.

Shelby & Supreme Butler: watching the two of you blossom has been the best thing in life. Every decision in my life is made with the two of you in mind.
Shelby, thank you for having the biggest heart a person can have. Thank you for ensuring that our relationship will forever have a close bond despite any situation life may bring us.
Supreme, your innocence is golden. I named you Supreme because it's (ranks the highest quality, degree and character a person can have). I know you will leave a Tremendous mark on this universe when it's all said and done. I love both of you and I hope I can make you proud.

Courtney Nicholson: Thank you for showing me better ways to express myself to others. One of the best pieces of advice I've received was you letting me know that being smart is searching for information to better yourself in this world. Reading the rough draft of this book to you and receiving your feedback was pure joy. I hope we continue to build what we have and one day write our own book together. You are the "Smartest" person I know and with a heart of Gold. Breezy.

TABLE OF CONTENTS

The Major Laws

Introduction

(pathos)
Thursday night 2002, Decatur Street, New Orleans, La.

I'm in the middle of the dance floor and all eyes are stuck on the legendary DJ doing one of his favorite sets. Jay-Z's voice fills the room "Drunk off Crist, mama on E, Can't keep her little model hands off me, both in the club, high singin' off-key." Then scratch-scratch, the music cuts to a part of a different song. Everyone in the club sang, "and I wish I never met her at all." That was the illest thing to a college kid whose life revolves around music and fashion. After taking DJ notes on a school night and driving an hour back to Nicholls State University, l had the confidence needed for my own Saturday night gig in Thibodaux, Louisiana.

(ethos)
One year later, I transitioned from behind the turntables to behind the microphone at KNSU the college station. I won

Best DJ of the Year awards and the support I received motivated me to create the first hip-hop hour in Lafourche Parish radio. During the summer of 2004, I interned at corporate station 104.5, where the same legendary DJ I'd taken notes from at the House of Blues was spinning. I had no car or money, and my mother was on her deathbed but I made it 104.5 every morning on time to work for free. I mainly assisted broadcasts; sometimes I rode in a small van to hang posters up in stores and watch my department boss do on-air calls at different locations. This was not fun for me. Although I did my job with pride and integrity, I just wanted to sneak into the actual studio and watch the DJs do the lunch and traffic mixes. I later got fired for spending too much time in there, not enough time shredding paper, and filling gift bags for radio callers. Nevertheless, everyone there knew that I was ready. One might ask, "for what?" I was ready to push the music culture alongside the tastemakers and key-holders in the city of New Orleans. With the help of the boss at the station, my readiness manifested. As a result, I became close friends and partners with that same legendary DJ who I drove city to city to watch perform and study.

Fortune cookie

Living in Los Angeles, California was life-changing for me. Not because of the weather, the palm trees, or the Lakers, it was my weekly trips to PF Chang's next to the Beverly Center that shaped my attitude. The fortune cookies at the end of each meal amazed me. *Every damn time* I ate there my cookie would read things like:

-You will be great in the entertainment world.
-You will be the creator of many things.
-Music will take you places you never dreamed of.

Crazy right? I would save them and drive my friends nuts talking about them. I would say, "I'm not listening to no one but these cookies." At that stage of my life, I did not understand the power of the universe -what we call signs, manifestation, God's plan, etc. You see, you must always keep your eyes open and ears clean in life because the universe is always talking to you. Hear it, understand it, and most importantly act on it. Two years after those moments at PF Chang's, I was later hired by many major label entertainment companies to do small jobs. Finally, I landed an amazing job at Atlantic Records. I then moved back home to run the New Orleans market for the label and strangely enough to work with those same people at the station I intern at. I even contracted some of them for events and other services.

Major Laws was creatively inspired by my journey and the power of the words from my fortune cookies. Hopefully, these principles can help your mentality and perspective daily. These principles were designed to bring your situations into a different light. For example, "the grass isn't always greener on the other side" is a well-known concept that has lasted for decades and still holds weight.

To get the most use out of this book, keep a highlighter on hand for parts that stand out to you.

You may also use a smartphone or a tablet to take notes on points that hit home with.

Words Are Seeds
We Should Plant Them

-Clean your room
-Wash your hands
-Go to bed at a decent hour
-Don't be late for school

I'm sure all of us have heard these demands from our parents growing up. We can agree in hindsight that it was some of the best and most helpful advice we've been given. Have you ever held a conversation with someone and it motivated or educated you afterwards and have you told yourself you will apply it to your life? Somehow those words sparked you or sometimes those conversations sit with you. I like to say they grow in you like a beautiful plant.

Some people are so blessed with a gift to speak to others' hearts and minds which causes that person to take actions after receiving those words. For example, former President Barack Obama was known for his amazing, heartfelt speeches. His words gave us hope and vision to see the change. Those seeds do not have to come from a president, a millionaire, or a college graduate. We can receive the words to plant inside of us from a coworker, family member, and friend. Just like planting a real plant, we must do the upkeep. Watering, checking sunlight time, and other things to see a plant blossom is the same way you upkeep the seeds you plant in your head. Let's say that seed was a business idea. The watering and upkeep would be you giving yourself mental progress reports like a checklist. Moving off seeds you plant in your head is very important, please do the proper upkeep to see that seed blossom and hopefully change your life for the better.

"Words Are SeedsWe Should Plant Them"

No One Forces You
To Stay In The Casino

Sometimes we blame others for our downfall or bad decisions we make. The most important thing in life as an adult I've learned is to blame the man in the mirror for many situations that turn out ugly.

-No one made you sign that bad contract.

-No one made you get into that toxic relationship.

-No one made you spend your last on something that wasn't essential.

-No one made you have unprotected sex.

These are the results of your actions. This isn't a religious book but I remember God gave us free will. We will miss a step or two or four or maybe seventeen but we must take accountability for those steps and keep moving.

"No One Forces You To Stay In The Casino "

Be A High End Fragrance Not An Odor

Nice guys always finish last is the biggest crap I've ever heard. Walking into a room with a smile, shaking hands, and asking people how their day is going can make someone's day. Being able to lend your ears to someone that needs to talk or vent can be so helpful. Most people don't forget you because of those moments. Kindness is important when searching for peace and receiving blessings. Never be the person that has more negative output than positive. Even when your day is not going well, still smile. It will brighten up the universe.

"Be A High End Fragrance Not An Odor"

Impossible Is A Big Word Created by Small People

-Jerry Rice birthplace, Starkville, Mississippi (Hall of Fame Receiver)

-Julia Roberts birthplace, Smyrna, Georgia (Award Winner Actress)

-Oprah Winfrey birthplace, Kosciusko, Mississippi (Oprah Network)

-Ellen DeGeneres birthday, Metairie, Louisiana (TV Host)

I'm positive the people on the list above had people from grade school discouraged them. Not because they didn't have what it took but sometimes doubters earn the name "hater" by simply not being able to see past the surface of their surroundings. Visionaries can see past the roof and behind the walls that others can't see. Hell Michael Jordan was cut from his high school team the first year he tried out and now look where he ended. Never listen to non-visionaries about your plans. Just keep pushing.

"Impossible Is A Big Word Created by Small People"

Stay Living To Stay Growing

Am I the only person that can look back into life and say that I came a long way? I was told that it takes twenty-eight days to kick a bad habit. I don't have the percentage on that theory but I can relate to it. All it takes is for you to wake up one morning, thank the higher powers and draw that line in the sand between the downfalls in your life and your future. Don't mix the two and *never* cross over the line that holds your downfalls. Like pops from the classic movie Friday would say, "win or lose just live to fight another day."

"Stay Living To Stay Growing"

Faith Is Mystery's Best Friend

Ask yourself how many times you had a bill due in a few days but had no idea how you were going to pay it, or an assignment that was due the next day and you hadn't even started it. When it was all said and done, the bill was paid and the task was completed. The mystery of tomorrow can scare those that suffer from lack of faith. When times get hard, it is mandatory for faith to take the wheel.
Sometimes you have to do your part and go to sleep while faith does the rest.

"Faith Is Mystery's Best Friend"

Don't Blame The Eskimo Blame The Wolf

Eskimos take sharp blades and cover it with blood from different types of animals. They will freeze the blood and add more. They repeat the steps a few times then plant the blade into the snow. When completed, the Eskimo's job is done, they hide and wait.. Eventually the wolf comes out to play and hunt. The wolf nose can easily pick up the scent of the blood and in minutes it discovers the bait. The wolf licks the blood *over* and *over*. The more blood it tastes, the more craving the wolf gets. Now licking for some time, the wolf is covered in blood and seems to get weaker by each lick. The wolf doesn't notice the blade and unfortunately doesn't notice it's actually eating its own blood. The wolf is licking the blade to the point that it's tongue is completely ripped off and in minutes the wolf will collapse and die.

Now I know we are not wolves and we don't lick blood off of sharp blades, but we do ultimately kill ourselves with an addiction of things that are no good for us. Sometimes we are blinded in worldly moments and indulge into pleasures. We are just being tricked by a false sense of happiness just like that hungry wolf, unable to see past that little taste that will end us for good. Don't let a 5 minute pleasure cost you a lifetime of pain.

"Don't Blame The Eskimo, Blame The Wolf"

Good People Roll With Good People
Smart People Roll With Smart People
Snakes Roll With Snakes

The quote explains itself. As kids our parents were always right about that one friend you brought home. Best advice is to keep your circle small. If you're rolling with three fools, then guess who's the fourth one?

"Good People Roll With Good People, Smart People Roll With Smart People, Snakes Roll With Snakes"

Once The Shit Get Bigger Than The Pet The Pet Must Go!

I was friends with someone for two decades. As teenagers we were close, but always had different views. Some say that makes for a better relationship, but not in this case. As adults our views became very different. Our relationship was filled with dark moments and bad energy. There were times we would even go months without speaking. At some point, I had to realize that the shit out-weighed the pet. We were having more dark times than bright times but notice, I didn't blame anyone in the situation because there's always three views to a situation.

Ask yourself how many relationships are you in due to the time of knowing that person. Are you having a shit show when you're around each other? Do conversations turn from good to bad in minutes or do you have to give yourself pep-talks before meeting up? If you've answered "yes" to any of these questions, then maybe it's time to get rid of the pet.

"Once The Shit Gets Bigger Than The Pet, The Pet Must Go"

Only Blind People Should Trip Over What's Behind Them

Once a decision has been made in your life, it's made. It may have been your call or the universe's, but the important part of moving on is actually moving on. After moving on from that job, that man, woman or business partner, a new vision should be created without them in it. You can't go back and forward with things in your past. The funniest thing with social media is we use it as a weapon or a courthouse. We may post pictures or tweet things that directly or indirectly speak to a situation from our past. How can we move forward and better ourselves if we still try to win old battles that truthfully have zero relevance to our life today? Remove the ego and pride, make your tomorrow better.

"Only Blind People Should Trip Over What's Behind Them"

Let People's Truth Be Their Truth

Question, have you ever lost your voice yelling at a friend, spouse or business partner during a debate to make your point? You can have all the information or evidence to support your point but that person will not change their view on the topic. Moments like that can ruin relationships. That was the story of my life until I understood that my view is my truth and that person's view is theirs.

A year ago I had to let certain people's truth be theirs. I attempted to describe the character of a loved one to their family but it was met with such force. I understood the situation was bigger than the matter at hand so I walked away from it to let them create the narrative that would give them the truth and peace they desire. Now the situation is unfolding just how I predicted but without me having to say one word. Deep inside I know the point was made. No more telling people their shirt is red if they say it's black, or that it's night if they say it's day time. We all see life through different lenses. Please keep in mind that it is okay to have different views, we are all different human beings.

"Let People's Truth Be Their Truth"

Quincy Jones Made Thriller At 50

There's no age limit on achieving greatness. Quincy Jones, a song writer and producer, approached living legend status early in his career. Hit after hit, award after award you would think someone with those achievements would slow down a little. Quincy knew something about himself that we definitely didn't know. He knew he had more to learn and give the world. At the age of 50, he partnered with a young artist named Michael Jackson and created the top selling record of all time "Thriller". For over thirty years, Thriller was number one.

Have you reached an age or time in your life where you feel your ceiling has closed or closing? Have you become bigger than your nine-to-five, or business? Do you feel as if you blew key opportunities to do something special? YOU ARE NOT DONE. Well at least we know age 50 isn't the deadline on being great. Each day you wake up is the day you can create your Thriller.

" Quincy Jones Made Thriller At 50"

God And Cannabis
Is All We Need

God

I would have never thought I could live without my
parents, especially my mother. After she passed away my
family was concerned about me. I was the youngest and
spoiled rotten so everyone thought I would shut down. I'm
not an usher boy but my faith is strong and I knew that
God only gave his hardest battles to his toughest soldiers.
Just a few weeks after her death, I moved to Los Angeles
to reprogram myself. God knew in order for me to put
down my childish acts and become a responsible person,
he would have to speak loudly to me. Now when I look
back at that year I always say that's the year I became a
man. Thanks to God.

How many times do you run into a problem that makes
you question everything but when it's over you look up to
the sky with a smile and say, "Ok God, I get it." I promise

you God is right next to you throughout every situation you face and he will always see you through and beyond it.

Cannabis

Depression is a disease that is fairly widespread without most people even knowing they have it. Another illness that goes unnoticed and untreated by most people is PTSD. PTSD doesn't just affect our veterans who served but any individual who experiences trauma. Some people like myself can go years and even decades without mourning tragic events in their life.

I was six feet away from my father when he took his last breath my junior year of high school. Two weeks after I was up and running because I played many sports. Fast forward to my sophomore year of college, I watched my mother fade away daily to cancer. Again I gave it no time, and a few weeks later I moved to Los Angeles to chase dreams. No moaning, healing or conversations. I told myself that life goes on but I was actually stuffing the pain away without letting it out.

Cannabis refers to a group of three plants with psychoactive properties known as Cannabis Sativa, Cannabis Indica and Cannabis Ruderalis.

Have You ever stepped back and took a look at your life? You see all of your self accomplishments, your beautiful family and all of the dope materialistic items you have but still find yourself in a dark space? I was 34-years-old when I realized I was filled with so much depression and PTSD (that's what my doctor called it). One day I was at my beautiful home, sitting in my beautiful backyard, overseeing the beautiful lake but my insides were full of pain. It was a really dark moment for me. That moment started to occur more and more until I realized I had to speak to someone. Escitalopram was prescribed to me but I hated the feeling. Yes, it was relaxing but in a nonproductive way. I work and create a lot so being asleep in bed from prescribed medication just didn't work for me.

Cannabis helped stabilize my moods when entering those dark moments but still kept me focused on my daily tabs. To all of my cannabis readers, is it true that you enjoy a good cannabis session after a long day of work or when you are trying your best to create something for the world? Add God to that plan and you can't be stopped.

"God And Cannabis Is All We Need

Learn To Unlearn

There was a young lady in the kitchen baking a ham. Her daughter asked her why she cut both ends of the ham before putting it into the oven. Her reply was, "I don't know, I watched my mother do it when I was a little girl ,so that's why I do it." Later that night that question popped into her head again, so she gave her mother a phone call. She asked her mother why she cut the ends off of the ham before putting it into the oven. Her mother's reply was, "because the oven was too small to fit the whole ham inside so I cut the edges." The young lady laughed and realized all those holidays she wasted good meat by doing what she saw her mother do and was unconsciously teaching her daughter the same.

Some generational teachings should not be passed down. Just because our fathers or mothers may abandon us, doesn't mean we can't be amazing parents. You can be a great husband despite watching your father cheat and mistreat your mother. Most of us have been taught something that maybe we shouldn't have been taught. Reprogramming your mind and views on life can do wonders. Everyday improvements are hard but needed.

"Learn To Unlearn"

Stop Giving The Devil More Credit Than God

We love to say "The devil is busy today" when we receive bad news about things in our life. Some people go even farther by saying "The devil made me do it". God hates that. You should turn your lens a little and view it differently. Maybe it was God that made you lose your job because he has a better one coming your way. The universe sends tests your way to see your reaction. Don't mention the devil's name when bad things appear at your door. A blessing can come knocking within a few seconds later. Trust your faith and higher powers not lower powers.

"Stop Giving The Devil More Credit Than God"

Always Use The Standing 8 Count

In professional boxing it's normal to see a boxer get knocked down. Successful boxers use the standing eight-count, eight seconds to reset after being knocked down, before continuing the match. Those seconds are vital because they help fighters refocus and gain their balance. Unfortunately, some boxers immediately hop back up and decline the eight seconds, setting themselves up to get knocked down once again. Unlikely after the second knock down they didn't get up. Their pride and ego made them rush the matter without regrouping. The standing eight-count method can be used in our everyday life. There have been many situations where we rush to judgment and may handle things wrongly with someone. We act off of pure emotions and don't give ourselves a standing eight to revisit the situation to confirm it. Most times standing back and viewing a situation from all sides really helps us.

"Always Use The Standing 8 Count"

Money Phones
Can't Be The End Goal

Peacocking is fine in my book. Some may say I'm
the peacock king. The flip side of that is knowing
the value of a dollar and investing it. I'm no
investment manager but I know if I have a closet
full of shoes and fabrics then I should have a good
credit score and plan for a better future. Nothing
is wrong with living in an apartment if we are
working towards purchasing a house. Nothing is
wrong with catching a bus if money is being
saved to purchase a vehicle. Have you ever sat
back and thought about all the unnecessary things
you bought for show instead of saving that money
for a better future? Sacrificing a $30 happy hour
once a week can land you $1560 at the end of the

year. That's a happy hour on an island for a weekend. Think bigger and you will do bigger things.

"Money Phones Can't Be The End Goal"

Apologizing Is A Strength Not A Weakness

Believe it or not, we become mentally stronger when we apologize to someone for things that may be our fault. Some feel like apologizing is a sign of weakness. There are so many of us holding onto guilt because we were too prideful to admit we are wrong. That ego and pride can cut so many blessings from coming our way.

Surprisingly, I've always said the worst part about the music business is the fame aspect. My job was to ensure the radio played my artist's records and sometimes I dealt with concert promoters who tried to cut my earnings. This can bring out the dark side of a person. Needless to say, I've done some things I regret. I started to view my past and was embarrassed. I was justified in many matters, but my quick temper took the situation to another level. I was forcing the other person to see the truth in the matter but I didn't realize "their truth was their truth".Three years ago during my peace breakthrough, I made my calls. I gave a few people in the industry an apology call. Some connections were from years ago that had likely faded away anyway.

Most important part about apologizing is to help yourself. It's not about restoring old relationships which is fine but more for the peace and clarity. Now you have put the ball into the receiver's hands and it's up to them to accept or decline, but you did your part. You are free of that situation and should never look back or be bothered by it again.

"Apologizing Is A Strength Not A Weakness"

Don't Compare Your Chapter 1 With Someone's Chapter 10

Do you think individuals like Michael Jackson, Bill Gates, and Russell Simmons woke up with an idea and two weeks later they were Rich and famous? I'm sure there were countless nights those guys had to work towards their goals. I've met lots of new artists who had goals to be huge stars, but they lacked the work ethic to achieve it. Greatness comes with dedication and working overtime. The first chapters of your journey should not be compared to someone further along on their journey. The smartest move to make is to have a conversation with that person and receive the knowledge from them. Most times that person can point you to your next move. So pay for those classes and networking seminars. When you're tired, suck it up and hit the few extra calls to promote your business. Push yourself then watch your life will change drastically.

"Don't Compare Your Chapter 1 With Someone's Chapter 10"

An Idle Mind Is The Devil's Playground

Every morning we wake up, we must have a plan. Since our minds are meant to think and create, it must always have a task. Look back on your life and ask yourself about the moments you put yourself in bad situations. Usually it stemmed from a negative thought instead of a positive one. The devil sits, waiting on our idle moments to hijack our brain and plant bad seeds that lead us down the wrong trail. We should always focus on righteous things, important things that benefit others and ourselves. Spend each day building your empire because an idle mind may cause everything you worked for to collapse.

"An Idle mind Is The Devils Playground"

Be Hungry Enough To Pass On A Cheap Meal

Far too many times we sign up for things out of excitement, ignorance and sometimes desperation. You can end up in bad relationships with someone because you both were seeking love and accepted the first person who said they wanted you. You may buy an overpriced vehicle or a run down apartment out of excitement. I've seen so many artists sign bad contracts because they lacked business education and saw a check in front of them with some zeros. Being patient is everything when it comes to elevating yourself. I haven't eaten pork since 2002. I can go hours without eating and may be starving but if someone offers me a ham sandwich I will respectfully decline because I know I will pay for it at the end of the day. Things in this world are not going anywhere, so there's no rush to achieve them. Take your time, learn yourself, educate yourself and make your moves wisely. A loaf of bread tastes a lot better than the remaining crumbs inside the bag.

"Be Hungry Enough To Pass On A Cheap Meal"

Life Throws Curve Balls But
We Still Have To Swing (Outro)

From 2008 till 2015, I had what one may call a "fun life." I traveled the world, working with famous people and making pretty good money. The entertainment business was all I knew. I thought I had it mastered but unfortunately it had me. I was a bad family member, bad husband, and father because those things were neither "fun or important" to me. Like I said before, God will speak to you and sometimes it can shake your world up. Leaving the company and working a nine-to-five felt like a punishment but it was not. I found myself during those times working to better myself. Now I can honestly say I'm a great friend, a great father and can't wait to show my future wife the unlimited love I have to give.

Some of the most beautiful farms across the world started with shit (literally). That manure was planted to create a beautiful harvest. Remember life is a marathon not a sprint. Take your time, put God and your peace first. Everything else will play itself out.

"Life Throws Curve Balls But We Still Have To Swing"

Love